Michiel Maandag is a
He is the founder of m
coaching and training b
creating brands that
about enough. His amb

Based on his experience working with global
brands and international marketing, Michiel has
invented unique and highly effective methods to
help create and maintain winning brands. This,
and his passion to make the complex simple, has directly led to the
ideas in *The Only Book You Will Ever Need on Branding*.

Michiel is Dutch and lives in the Netherlands with his Finnish
wife and their daughter.

Read more at www.michielmaandag.com or reach him at
michiel@mondaybrand.com

Liisa Puolakka is a director of research and
strategy at ChauhanStudio, a boutique industrial
design practise. She is former head of Nokia's
global brand identity.

When Michiel Maandag, a colleague during
her time at Nokia, got in touch to suggest writing
a book together, she jumped at the opportunity.
She is allergic to marketing jargon and complex
models, always driven to find a different, unique
angle to things – like this no-nonsense brand book for businesses.
A fashion designer by degree, she illustrates for fun. Her next big
goal is to launch a baby toy brand that meticulously follows all the
guidance of *The Only Book You Will Ever Need on Branding*!

Liisa is Finnish and lives in London with her husband and two
daughters.

Reach her at liisa@liisapuolakka.com

THE ONLY BOOK YOU WILL EVER NEED ON BRANDING

to start, run and grow your business

MICHIEL MAANDAG & LIISA PUOLAKKA

A How To Book

ROBINSON

ROBINSON

First published in Great Britain in 2014 by
CreateSpace Independent Publishing Platform
This paperback edition published in 2015 by Robinson

A CIP catalogue record for this book
is available from the British Library.

ISBN 978-1-47213-607-7 (paperback)

3 5 7 9 8 6 4 2
Typeset in Great Britain by Mousemat Design Limited
Printed and bound in Great Britain by CPI Group (UK) Ltd, Croydon CR0 4YY
Papers used by Robinson are from well-managed forests and other
responsible sources

Robinson
is an imprint of
Little, Brown Book Group
Carmelite House
50 Victoria Embankment
London EC4Y 0DZ

An Hachette UK Company
www.hachette.co.uk

www.littlebrown.co.uk

How To Books are published by Robinson, a part of Little, Brown Book Group. We
welcome proposals from authors who have first-hand experience of their subjects.
Please set out the aims of your book, its target market and its suggested contents
in an email to Nikki.Read@howtobooks.co.uk

Contents

This book is about how – not why.

Read it and branding will be a breeze.

1
A GOOD BRAND MAKES GOOD BUSINESS

Whatever you are selling – a product, an experience, a cause – there needs to be something that captures and marks everything you do, so people can talk about 'it', recognize 'it' and buy 'it'.

That 'it' is your brand.

You cannot sell or promote without a brand.

It is that important.

2
WHAT IS A BRAND?

A BRAND IS A NAME THAT, IN THE MIND OF A CONSUMER, IS ATTACHED TO A PRODUCT CATEGORY.

In the mind of the consumer, Heinz is attached to the ketchup category.

In the mind of the consumer, Coca-Cola is attached to the cola drink category.

In the mind of the consumer, WhatsApp is attached to the free texting category.

In the mind of the consumer, Google is attached to the search category.

HOW DO YOU GET YOUR BRAND ATTACHED TO A PRODUCT CATEGORY IN THE MIND OF A CONSUMER?

**This is what the rest of the book
will tell you...**

3
HOW TO POSITION YOUR BRAND

You position your brand by defining who it is for and what it does.

Like this:

Coca-Cola is the only cola drink that helps everyone to experience the authentic cola taste, so that they feel refreshed in their mind, body and spirit.

THE BRAND POSITIONING FORMULA:

__(Your brand)_____ is the only

__(your product category)_____

that helps __(your target audience)_____

to __(what your brand is used for)__

so that __(why your target audience__

__uses your brand)_____

Like this:

__Facebook_____ is the only

__social network_____

that helps __everyone_____

to __connect and share with_____

__the people they choose_____

so that __they can give and get_____

__instant attention._____

A brand has **one positioning**.

A brand has **one positioning statement**.

Once established, you have to stick with it, because even if you don't, your consumers will...

_____BRAND_____ is the only

_____

that helps _____

to _____

so that _____ .

For example, the Volkswagen Group bought **Škoda** in 1991, an automobile manufacturer based in the Czech Republic.

It has been busy ever since changing the brand positioning of **Škoda** away from what was established in the mind of European consumers as 'a very low quality vehicle, completely lacking the credibility of a modern car brand'.

Why? What value to the new car did the brand name **Škoda** add?

It would have been much easier and much cheaper to create a new brand without the bad history and with a name that would add a positive perception of origin. Cars from Germany versus cars from the Czech Republic are perceived very differently.

It is not what you say your brand is, it is what consumers say it is. There is no point fighting an established consumer perception.

4
WHAT IS YOUR PRODUCT CATEGORY?

You must attach your brand to a product category to give it meaning. Without a clear category it is hard to say what you are.

Facebook is a **social network**.

Heinz is a **ketchup**.

iPhone is a **smartphone**.

_____ is the only

CATEGORY

that helps _____

to _____

so that _____ .

IF YOU DON'T TELL

WHAT YOUR PRODUCT

CATEGORY IS,

THEN OTHERS WILL.

With the introduction of the Galaxy Note in 2011, Samsung left the product category out from the advertisement. To describe the product Samsung used the headline: 'Phone? Tablet? It's Galaxy Note!'.

As a result, bloggers had to invent the category name. The term **phablet** was born.

Clearly say what you are, so people can talk about you without having to invent a category name for you.

Journalist:

'Today we are with the founder of WhatsApp, the number one **free messaging app**...'

User:

'I use a **free messaging app** for that, check out WhatsApp.'

Wikipedia.org:

'The iPad is a line of **tablet computers** designed and marketed by Apple Inc.'

'Smart Automobile is an automotive branch of Daimler AG that specialises in manufacturing **microcars**.'

5

ATTACH YOUR BRAND TO ONE CATEGORY

A brand is strongest in the mind of the consumer when it has only one meaning.

Mitsubishi uses one brand name for all of its product categories. So, what is Mitsubishi?

It is a brand that stands for anything from **IT services to cars, to water and power business, to metals and chemicals**. For a consumer it is unclear what Mitsubishi is.

Mercedes-Benz is still in the mind of the consumer a **luxury German car**, but for how long?

In the UK the cheapest cars they now offer start from £20,715 – the price level of Toyotas – well below luxury car brand prices. This makes Mercedes-Benz's positioning vulnerable and leaves room for a real and focused luxury car brand to step in.

IN THE MIND OF THE CONSUMER, A BRAND THAT DOES JUST ONE THING REALLY WELL IS MORE CREDIBLE THAN A BRAND THAT DOES EVERYTHING.

Mitsubishi would be much more credible in **chemicals**, if that were the only thing they did.

Mercedez-Benz would not risk losing their credibility as a **luxury German car**, if they stuck to making expensive cars.

Would you prefer to take your BMW to the KwikFit body shop or the brand approved one?

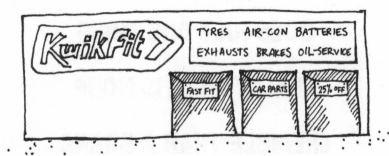

FOCUS

It helps to define the product category by narrowing down until you find the one thing that is unique, real and that your brand can truly own.

This way you can come up with a completely new category, and being the first, the inventor, gives you a great competitive advantage.

For example, the Toyota corporation invented the luxury Japanese car category, when they launched Lexus. They narrowed down from Japanese cars to **luxury Japanese cars**, a unique product category nobody owned or occupied.

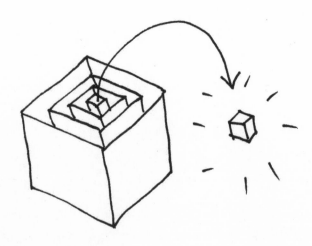

In the mind of the mass consumer:

Dyson invented the **bagless vacuum cleaner** category.

Google invented the **search** category.

Tesla invented the **luxury electric car** category.

Ella's Kitchen invented the **baby food pouches** category.

Uber invented the **mobile-app-based taxi service** category.

Vanessa Mae invented the **violin-techno-acoustic-fusion** category.

You know that you own a category in the mind of the consumers, when your brand becomes synonymous with it.

For example: 'Google it!'
For searching the Internet

'Do you have the thermos?'
For a vacuum flask

'Just photoshop it!'
For photo manipulation

'Could you hand me a band-aid?'
For a plaster

'Please could you hoover here?'
For vacuum cleaning

However, even though the adopted word stays in the language, this is no guarantee of the future sales. Many leading brands have lost their relevance due to products that failed to evolve and meet the future requirements of their customers.

6

WHO IS YOUR BRAND FOR?

Whether you target a narrow or broad audience, be clear about who your brand is for. Stay true to your target.

Don't try to be different things to different audiences.

_____ is the only

_____

that helps **TARGET**

to _____

so that _____ .

For example:

To consumers Philips is an electronics company. To businesses and organisations Philips is more of a healthcare device manufacturer.

So, what is Philips? According to their website, Philips is 'a diversified technology company, focused on improving people's lives through meaningful innovation in the areas of Healthcare, Consumer Lifestyle and Lighting'. Needless to say, target audiences are confused and the Philips brand is being diluted.

What should Philips have done?

To keep things clear for their different audiences, the company should have kept the Philips brand focused in the consumer electronics category and created a new brand for the healthcare category.

Philips electronics

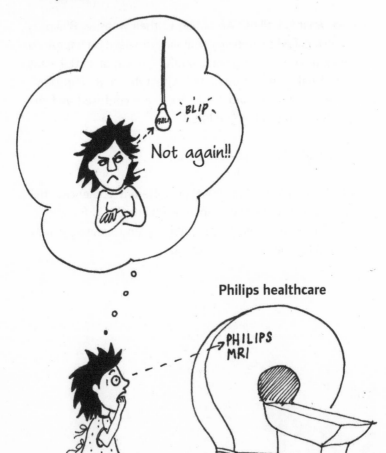

Philips healthcare

IF YOU TRY TO BE EVERYTHING TO EVERYBODY, YOU WILL BECOME NOTHING TO NOBODY.

7
WHAT IS YOUR BRAND USED FOR?

Think about the concrete things your target audience tries to achieve with your brand — what exactly do they use it for?

These are the unique benefits you offer to your consumers.

These are the things you should do better than anyone else.

_____ is the only
_____
that helps _____
to _____ WHAT _____
so that _____ .

For example:

People **buy anything and everything, quickly and conveniently**, at Amazon – the world's largest online retailer.

People **experience the authentic cola taste** by drinking Coca-Cola.

People **clean, moisturize and deodorize** their skin **gently** with Dove's products.

People **dress up in sports fashion** with Nike's stylish gear.

These sneakers are so cool...

8

WHY DOES YOUR TARGET AUDIENCE USE YOUR BRAND?

Your target audience buys your brand because it makes them feel a certain way.

The effect your brand has should fulfill a deep, underlying human need.

_____ is the only

_____

that helps _____

to _____

so that ___WHY___.

For example:

In the crowded **personal care** category, Dove changed the rules by focusing on feelings over product: be happy with who you are, focus on what you have, there are no flaws.

Since the Real Beauty Campaign started in 2004, Dove continues to focus on its unique positioning to build 'a world where beauty is a source of confidence, and not anxiety.' (www.dove.us).

The complete positioning statement could be:

Dove is the only personal care product that helps men and women clean, moisturize and deodorize their skin gently, **so that they can be confident in their bodies and look good, no matter who they are**.

The underlying human need for buying Nike is not to get a better performing sneaker, but to bring out the cool and dynamic athlete in themselves – an image that Nike has so successfully created through the endorsement of the world's best athletes.

Nike's complete positioning statement could be:

Nike is the only sports brand that helps people to dress up in sports fashion, **so that they can express the attitude and style of a celebrity athlete on the streets or in the gym and make themselves feel more attractive**.

<u>9</u>

EVERYTHING COMES TOGETHER IN YOUR PRODUCT

Your product is the absolute manifestation of your positioning.

Always keep it that way.

Your positioning **will** deteriorate if you don't, leaving room for competition to come in and take what was yours!

Porsche is the **iconic sports car**.

Yet, in 2014, only 29% of Porsche's sales were true sports cars and 58% were SUVs.

What does that mean for Porsche's future? The youth will learn that Porsche is an SUV brand. Porsche will become a diluted car brand as more focused companies take the sports car segment.

Porsche should have created a new brand for the SUVs, just like Toyota created Lexus for their line of luxury cars.

Google is **the search engine**.

Financially, Google is all about search. In the results from 2003 to 2014 the percentage of advertising revenue of Google's total revenue has been 89% or more.

Yet Google is extending its brand into many other categories with Google Maps, Google Play, Google Drive, Google News, Google Calendar, Google Translate, Google Books, Google Offers, Google Wallet, Google Shopping, Google+, Google Earth, Google Glass and much more.

The google.com user interface started to suffer, when they tried to integrate all the extensions on the home page. Google was fast becoming a brand in search of a clear positioning and focus.

In Autumn 2013 Google refocused the google.com user interface on search. Google's next challenge is to continue to innovate in the search category.

Google should keep focus by linking only search related products to the brand Google and keep the non-search products separate.

Just like Android and YouTube that Google acquired. Or Gmail. Because consumers access YouTube directly and 'go to Gmail'.

Once upon a time...

Then it all changed...

The good old times are back!

Mini is a **small car built for 'adventurers, thinkers, creators, free spirits, lovers and fighters against the conventional'**.

Mini's portfolio fully reflects its brand positioning. Firstly, the different models are instantly recognizable as quirky Minis. Secondly, only a few Minis on the road are exactly the same. There is a vast number of options available to help consumers to customize their cars and be those 'free spirits'.

POSITIONING = PRODUCT.

PRODUCT = POSITIONING.

ALWAYS.

10

EXPAND YOUR BUSINESS, NOT YOUR BRAND

Don't let your focused brand limit the growth of your business. Create a new brand for a new category.

For example:

'Levi Strauss Casual' or a 'Levi's Khaki' would never play a role in the **business casual clothing** category, but Dockers has since 1986.

'Toyota Luxe' at $50,000 would never play a role in the **luxury Japanese car** category, but Lexus has since 1989.

'Black & Decker Professional' would never play a role in the **professional tools** category, but DeWalt (a Black & Decker company) has since 1992.

'Nokia Pearl' at €5,000 would never play a role in the **luxury phone** category, but Vertu (originally a Nokia company) has since 1998.

Yet companies keep launching new categories under brand names with an already established positioning. This creates conflict and confusion in the minds of their loyal customers, and at the same time diminishes the credibility of the products in the new category.

For example:

Red Bull launched 'Red Bull Cola', an **all natural cola**. Established in 2008, it discontinued distribution in the USA in 2011.

Why?

The concept of an all natural cola is good. It is the answer to the growing trend of going natural. Unfortunately, this is in conflict with the Red Bull positioning. **Red Bull** is, in consumers' minds, the **number one energy drink**. Secondly, energy drinks are far from natural and contain synthetic taurine.

Instead, Red Bull should have created a new brand to capture the all natural cola category.

Land Rover is known for its **robust four-wheel-drive SUVs**.

Today however Land Rover has stretched into bicycles. Why? Land Rover should focus its time and energy on selling more SUVs rather than bicycles.

ONE POSITIONING

ONE MEANING

ONE BRAND

If you still believe you should stretch your brand into new product categories, use the **Flip Test** to find out if consumers can make the stretch... and buy more of your brand.

For example, if your brand and category is **Angry Birds mobile games** and you want to see whether consumers could make the stretch and buy **Angry Birds children's books**...

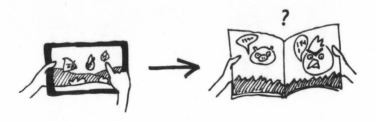

...**flip it!** Take an established brand in the **children's books** like **Pip and Posy** and extend it to your category of **mobile games**.

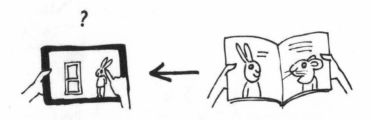

Then ask yourself... **does this make sense?** Yes. So in this case the brand Angry Birds could extend into children's books.

Current: Red Bull energy drink
Extension: Red Bull cola

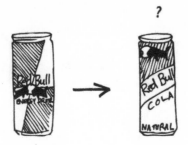

Flip it!
Current: Pepsi cola drink
Extension: Pepsi energy drink

Does this make sense? No. So Red Bull should not
have extended into cola drinks.

Current: Black & Decker power tools
Extension: Black & Decker electric kettle

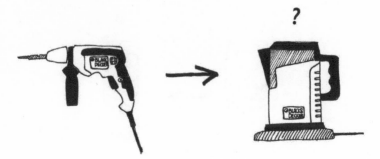

Flip it!
Current: DeLonghi electric kettle
Extension: DeLonghi power tools

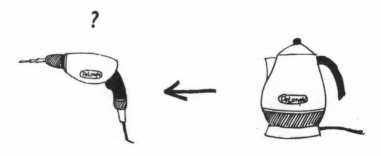

Does this make sense? No. So Black & Decker should
not have extended into kettles.

FLIP...

BEFORE YOU STRETCH

YOUR BRAND.

11

A BAD NAME REMAINS A BAD NAME

FOREVER.
UNLESS YOU CHANGE IT.

Jennifer Aniston or Jennifer Anastassakis?

Demi Moore or Demetria Guynes?

Marilyn Monroe or Norma Jeane Baker?

Lady Gaga or Stefani Germanotta?

CINEMA

JENNIFER	ANASTASSAKIS	
DEMETRIA	GUYNES	
	NORMA JEANE BAKER	
	STEFANI GERMANOTTA	

Fixing a bad name with a better product, better messaging or more marketing will leave you nowhere, except heading towards bankruptcy.

Follow Ralph Lifshitz and change a bad name. And look what happened to **Ralph Lauren**.

DESCRIPTIVE
BRAND NAMES
ARE ALWAYS BAD.

Descriptive names are never unique. They just describe: car, bookstore, radio, app, social network, blogger...

Imagine the following conversation:

'I just downloaded **Meetings**'
'You downloaded meetings ???'
'The **Meetings** app!'
'Which Meetings app?'
'**Meetings**!'
'There are two Meetings apps in the app store, which one do you mean?'
'Eh... it is called **Meetings**, let me see...' Etc.

Versus:

'I use the **Miss Moneypenny** app for my meetings and it is great!'

Need more evidence?

There are no descriptive brand names on the Interbrand Top 100 World's Most Valuable Brands list.

12
THE SIX CS FOR A GOOD NAME

CRISP

CLEAR

CLEVER

CONNECTED

CONVERSATIONAL

CRAZY

The six Cs give you a framework that helps you to come up with a good and memorable brand name.

They are not rules and your brand name does not need to fulfil all six Cs.

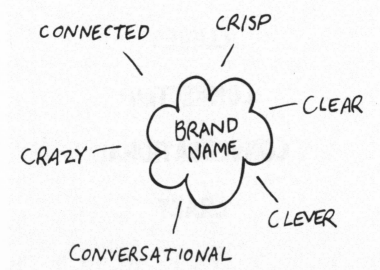

Crisp

Keep it short and sweet.

In general, short names are easier to remember, to spell and to say.

For example:

FedEx versus Federal Express
Mac versus Macintosh
Amex versus American Express

CLEAR

When CSA (Consumers See an Acronym) for the first time, they will try to figure out what the acronym stands for.

Instead, consumers should spend their energy learning what your brand stands for and linking the name with the product category.

Many consumers still don't know what these letters stand for:

AKG, AMD, ARM, B&H, BT, CBS, CVS, DKNY, FTD, GNC, JAL, SAS, TWA, etc.

Speed up your success and do not create acronyms.

CLEVER

Associate the brand name with the product category:

Twitter – birds tweeting – sending short messages

WordPress – pressing words – a blogging platform

Amazon – the world's biggest river – the world's largest online retailer

And possibly with your main benefit as well:

Budget – money conscious – 'Renting great cars to value-minded customers since 1958'

CONVERSATIONAL

A brand name that is easy for anyone to pronounce – and to talk about without fear of embarrassment – has an advantage. Some brand names can look interesting, but are difficult to pronounce.

For example:

Fage yoghurt
Kinerase skin care company
Peugeot car company
Givenchy fashion

Other names can look unique on paper, but lose their uniqueness when pronounced.

For example:

'Gruupz' app is pronounced as descriptive 'groups'.

CONNECTED

Brand names consisting of multiple words are much easier to remember when they are connected using alliteration.

For example:

Bed, Bath & Beyond
Best Buy
PayPal
Dunkin' Donuts
BlackBerry
Firefox
American Airlines
American Apparel

CRAZY

Boring names don't cut it, whereas unexpected names in their respective product categories can do miracles.

For example:

BlackBerry for business phones
Google for search
Penguin for a book publisher
P Diddy for a rapper

13
WHAT IF YOU CAN'T GET YOURBRANDNAME.COM?

In general .com domains are still the best, because that is what most consumers will try first when looking for a brand website.

If your desired domain name is not yet registered, then don't think twice and get it immediately.

However, with only a few letters in the alphabet, most names are already taken.

When you can't purchase the .com domain that you want, then there are a couple of options available.

Construct your domain by adding the product category after the name:

yourname**app**.com
yourname**wine**.com
yourname**toy**.com

Most country domain extensions are now available to anyone, so you can use them creatively:

.am for -am ending, like **instagr.am**
.be for -be endings, like **youtu.be**
.fm for radio, like **last.fm**
.me for me phrases, like **join.me**
.us for us or -ious phrases, like **donttrack.us** or **delicio.us**

Keep in mind that shorter domain names are best. For example airbnb.com was a vast improvement from airbedandbreakfast.com.

14
HOW TO CREATE A GOOD LOGO

PEOPLE NOTICE

FIRST A SHAPE,

THEN A COLOUR

AND LASTLY CONTENT

– LIKE TEXT.

Every brand needs a logo. Your aim is to make the logo recognizable on its own and to represent everything your brand stands for.

Create one of the following types of logos:

1. The brand name alone, unframed or framed

2. The brand name plus a symbol

1. The brand name alone

This works particularly well when you have a short brand name, because a short brand name can have a very strong shape as it is, like IBM.

Unframed examples:

Framed examples:

2. The brand name plus a symbol

This type works particularly well for longer brand names. The symbol gives an easily recognizable shape that a long name lacks. It can also emphasize the meaning or category of your brand, like WhatsApp + speech bubble.

WhatsApp

Avoid using the symbol on its own, because there are new consumers born everyday and they need to learn that your symbol equals your brand, like the swoosh equals Nike or the mermaid equals Starbucks.

WHEN PEOPLE SEE YOUR LOGO FOR THE FIRST TIME, DON'T MAKE THEM WONDER WHAT THE BRAND NAME IS. PUT IT ON THE LOGO.

It's important to ensure that your logo can be used across different media.

For example in mobile devices and in any social media, your logo will have to fit into a very limited space, usually the size of a profile image. For a longer brand name this creates legibility issues, and that's where the symbol becomes very useful.

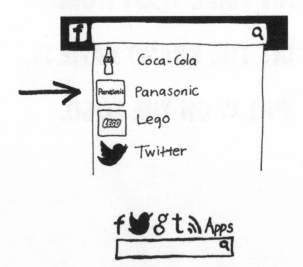

Keep the following in mind when creating a logo:

1. Design your logo to last forever – get it right the first time and then stick with it.

2. Create something completely unique – do your research, especially among competition.

3. Text should be easy to read – keep it horizontal.

4. The logo should function anywhere and on all kinds of backgrounds – keep it simple in shape and colour and make sure it also works in black and white.

5. If you have a brand slogan, you should create a version of your logo with the slogan attached – never use the slogan without the brand logo.

6. The logo should be appropriate to your business and target audience – ensure it expresses your positioning and that it's not in conflict with any relevant cultural issues.

7. Test, test and test before you launch – can you enlarge and reduce the size of the logo, does it work across different media? Most importantly, does it express your brand the way it should?

8. Many brand logos evolve over time, often to become visually simpler. If your logo is already established, make only incremental changes, so that the recognizability of the brand is never jeopardized.

Creating a logo is not an easy task – it requires a lot of creativity, consideration and practical knowledge. If you are not a designer, then hire a professional to create the logo for you and use these eight steps to brief him or her.

15
HOW TO OWN A COLOUR

Your primary goal is to use your brand colour so consistently that you start to own it in your category.

Like UPS brown, Ikea blue and yellow, Cadbury purple or Harrods green. It is even possible to trademark a brand colour. For example, Tiffany has protected their blue colour.

MAKE PEOPLE THINK OF YOUR BRAND WHEN THEY SEE A COLOUR.

Keep the following in mind when choosing brand colours:

1. Keep it simple – too many colours makes using them hard and the recognition of your brand by colour even harder. One or two core colours are required for a logo, and these colours should also become the visual identifiers across different media: website, packaging, brochures, advertising, uniforms, vehicles, even buildings.

2. The colours need to complement each other, yet have good contrast, so that the details stand out clearly and the legibility is enhanced.

3. Be distinctive – check the colours your competition is using.

4. Test, test and test – how do the colours look on screen and in print, are there any cultural issues, are there any technical issues with reproducing the colours, do they stand out on different backgrounds?

5. Most importantly, just like the logo, your colours need to express and enhance the meaning of your brand, have relevance to your audience and **last for a long time**.

Once you have established your brand colours, resist the urge to change for the sake of change!

16
You Can Own More Than Just The Logo And Colours

You can develop and own more assets to help your consumers identify and be reminded of your brand. They could be, for example, fonts, jingles or design details on your products.

These assets can become extremely valuable and make you stand out and be instantly recognizable – but **only** if used consistently.

Examples of famous brand assets:

'Intel inside' jingle
BMW's kidney shaped grille
Nokia's default ringtone
Virgin's mischievous and fun tone of voice
UPS's brown vans and employee uniforms
Levi's red tab
Mini Babybel cheese shape
Coca-Cola's glass bottle
Ikea's 'blue box' building

But remember – with a good logo and a couple of core colours you can get far.

USE YOUR IDENTITY CONSISTENTLY FOR AS LONG AS THE BRAND LIVES. WHEN YOU OR YOUR AGENCY GETS BORED, YOUR CONSUMERS HAVE JUST STARTED TO LEARN!

17
TELL YOUR STORY

There is nothing better than a true brand story, because it is unique and it is **yours**. Your story is about **why** and **how** you you started your brand. It gives an authentic foundation to what you are selling.

In the short term your story is your ticket to the media. A good story gives a unique and fresh angle to an existing or new product category – it is something interesting to write about.

Eventually, your brand story is the long term differentiator against the competition. This is why you want to keep reminding people about it – so they feel good about picking your brand over the competition.

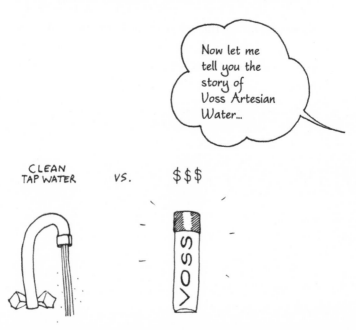

For example:

Firefox, the open-source web browser, launched in 2004 as a true alternative to Microsoft's Internet Explorer.

Their story was all about the power of community versus corporate creation. 'At its core, Firefox is about people and is powered by a global community of individuals working together for the public good.' It showed the strength of their story that Firefox's first advertisement in the *New York Times* was funded by its fans!

Unfortunately, over the years their community story has got lost among many other stories and messages. As a result, the unique and original Firefox story is no longer a differentiator in the mind of the consumer. It is no longer the reason to select Firefox over the competition and for most consumers Firefox has become just another browser.

**KEEP YOUR STORY ALIVE.
IT IS THE ONE THING
NOBODY CAN COPY.**

18
MAKE PEOPLE TALK ABOUT YOU

It is not the things you do better or different from your competition that make people talk about you – it is the things that you do that are **new**.

When you introduce a new product category, you always have a great opportunity to be newsworthy.

When you compete within an established product category, you still have to keep providing something new.

For example, hardly anyone is waiting to see what is better in the next iPhone, everybody is just eagerly waiting for what is new. Apple has introduced, since the launch of the first iPhone in 2007, one big new thing every year and kept interest around the iPhone high.

FOCUS ON WHAT IS NEW.

19
YOUR SLOGAN SUMS UP YOUR BRAND

A slogan is a memorable phrase that is the summary of your brand.

A good slogan always describes your product and its unique benefit. A really good slogan will set you above the competition and ultimately create a reason for people to buy **your** brand.

Good examples:

M&M's – Melts in your mouth, not in your hands

Evernote – Remember everything

BMW – The ultimate driving machine

HSBC – The world's local bank

Bad examples:

Heineken – Open your world
(Is beer your world? That's a bit sad.)

Philips – Let's make things better
(The current products are not good?)

Chevrolet – Find new roads
(People don't find new roads in a Ford?)

20
BE
CONSISTENT
WHEN YOU
COMMUNICATE

Use consistent messages to establish your positioning. Once established, keep your messages consistent to reinforce your positioning. Your positioning should not change over time, so the core of your messages should not change either.

Today, focus is more important than ever because on the Internet everything is kept forever – including the inconsistent messages – endangering your established positioning.

When your marketing team or agency gets fed up with the repetition, use this book to explain its importance.

Or fire them.

Let's do something different!!

EVERY INCONSISTENT MESSAGE IS A MESSAGE THAT HARMS YOUR BRAND. REPEAT, REPEAT AND REPEAT.

Why does the world buy Coca-Cola?

Because it is the real thing!

After all, you can't beat the real thing.

But the only consistent thing about Coca-Cola slogans since 1886 has been that they change. CocaCola should instead capitalize on their distinctiveness and keep repeating the message that 'it's the real thing' – reinforcing the positioning.

DRINK COCA-COLA. DELICIOUS AND REFRESHING. COCA-COLA REVIVES AND SUSTAINS. THE GREAT NATIONAL TEMPERANCE BEVERAGE. GOOD TIL THE LAST DROP. THREE MILLION A DAY. THIRST KNOWS NO SEASON. ENJOY LIFE. REFRESH YOURSELF. SIX MILLION A DAY. IT HAD TO BE GOOD TO GET WHERE IT IS. PURE AS SUNLIGHT. AROUND THE CORNER FROM ANYWHERE. COCA-COLA ... PURE DRINK OF NATURAL FLAVORS. ICE-COLD SUNSHINE. AMERICA'S FAVORITE MOMENT. THE BEST FRIEND THIRST EVER HAD. COCA-COLA GOES ALONG. COCA-COLA IS COKE! THE ONLY THING LIKE COCA-COLA IS COCA-COLA ITSELF. HOW ABOUT A COKE. FOR PEOPLE ON THE GO. THINGS GO BETTER WITH COKE. COKE ... AFTER COKE ... AFTER COKE. I'D LIKE TO BUY THE WORLD A COKE. HAVE A COKE AND A SMILE. **IT'S THE REAL THING.** COKE IS IT! AMERICA'S REAL CHOICE. CATCH THE WAVE. ALWAYS COCA-COLA. LOVE IT LIGHT. MAKE IT REAL. **CAN'T BEAT THE REAL THING.** CAN'T BEAT THE FEELING. THE COKE SIDE OF LIFE. OPEN HAPPINESS. LIFE BEGINS HERE. THE COLD CRISP TASTE OF COKE. ENJOY COCA-COLA.

Volvo is still in the mind of the consumer the 'world's safest car'. However, they are quickly losing this as their current vision is 'to be the world's most progressive and desired luxury car brand'. The word 'safety' is not even included.

Volvo really had the best positioning in the car category. Sure, all cars are safe, but who does not want to have the safest car?

Volvo is giving their unique and hard-earned positioning away to try to get into a category already occupied by the likes of Audi or Mercedes-Benz.

MasterCard has kept communications consistent since 1997 with their 'Priceless' campaign and the core message: 'There are some things money can't buy. For everything else, there's a MasterCard.' While the campaign has evolved to stay fresh and relevant to the MasterCard audiences, it has always stayed true to the core message.

MasterCard has publicly spoken about their commitment to engage with the consumers in a way that is consistent with their brand positioning, and how their research has assured them that there is no need to change – people are not getting tired of the campaign.

Their communications strategy has been so successful that every year since the launch of 'Priceless' the revenue and brand value of MasterCard has grown steadily. During the Grammy Awards in 2014 the hashtag #PricelessSurprises rose to the number 5 trending topic on Twitter.

21
COMPETE THROUGH COMMUNICATION

If you are the leader in your category, then say that you are. This makes others look like copycats.

Coca-Cola, **the real thing**.
There can only be one real cola drink, and the real thing is better than an alternative.

Heinz, **the world's favourite ketchup**.
There can only be one world's favorite, and that is better than an alternative.

Once you are the first in the mind of the consumer, it is hard to convince consumers otherwise. Even if another ketchup brand would sell better than Heinz, consumers would still believe for a long time that Heinz is the number one in the ketchup category.

When you compete against the category leader, present yourself as the true alternative.

Apple used the 'Mac vs PC' commercials to present itself as a true alternative to Windows PCs. It did that by addressing the flaws of Windows PCs that were **acknowledged** by Windows users and potential buyers. This made the commercial a success.

Microsoft is taking a similar approach with the 'Surface vs iPad' commercials. For example, Microsoft suggests that not being able to run two apps next to each other on the screen is a major flaw, however the current tablet users have **not acknowledged** this. Therefore, Microsoft has failed to present itself as a credible alternative and their marketing campaign is unlikely to succeed.

PRESENT YOURSELF AS THE TRUE ALTERNATIVE USING THE ACKNOWLEDGED FLAWS OF THE CATEGORY LEADER.

22
LET PEOPLE AND AND TRUSTED MEDIA BUILD YOUR BRAND

CONSUMERS

DO NOT TRUST

ADVERTISING.

Gallup releases annual figures of the image of certain professions ranked by honesty and ethics. In 2014, the bottom three in the USA were **advertising practitioners**, **members of congress** and **car salespeople**.

How would you rate the honesty and ethical standards of people in these different fields?

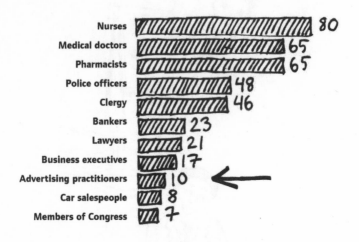

Source: Gallup Dec. 8–11, 2012

To what extent do you trust the following forms of advertising?

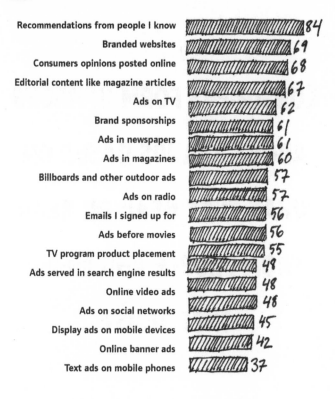

% Completely / Somewhat trust

Recommendations from people I know	84
Branded websites	69
Consumers opinions posted online	68
Editorial content like magazine articles	67
Ads on TV	62
Brand sponsorships	61
Ads in newspapers	61
Ads in magazines	60
Billboards and other outdoor ads	57
Ads on radio	57
Emails I signed up for	56
Ads before movies	56
TV program product placement	55
Ads served in search engine results	48
Online video ads	48
Ads on social networks	48
Display ads on mobile devices	45
Online banner ads	42
Text ads on mobile phones	37

Source: Nielsen Global Survey of Trust in Advertising, Q1 2013

CONSUMERS FORM OPINIONS ABOUT BRANDS BASED ON WHAT THEY HEAR OR READ FROM PEOPLE AND MEDIA THEY TRUST.

When was the last time you bought a car **just** based on advertising?

Decisions about cars are based on what people see and **hear** from friends, family or colleagues and what they **read** in the reviews. Only after that do they book a test drive.

Or did you go out and see a movie **just** based on the TV trailer and the street posters?

People choose a movie based on what they **hear** from friends and what they **read** from the reviews.

Get out, find and contact the blogs, review sites, newspapers and magazines that would be interested in writing about your brand and the story behind it.

In return you get a credible voice helping you to build your brand and attach it to a product category.

23

USE ADVERTISING TO PROTECT YOUR POSITIONING

Once you are an established brand, the bloggers, review sites and newspapers will be less interested in writing about you. Unless you continue to provide substantially new products, features or stories, you will become old news fast.

When you are an established brand with few stories to tell, you need to turn to advertising to protect your brand and to maintain its position, like Google who has only recently turned to advertising to protect its position in Search.

What should you advertise?

Focus on your leadership position with your product and its unique benefit. This is usually captured in your slogan.

For example:

Gillette – the best a man can get

Ajax – stronger than dirt

Google – the #1 search engine
(Unfortunately, Google is not actually saying that.)

24
ALL YOUR ACTIONS NEED TO REFLECT YOUR POSITIONING

EVERY INCONSISTENT ACTION IS AN ACTION THAT HARMS YOUR BRAND.

All your actions and interactions with your customers must be consistent with your brand positioning. This includes the user-friendliness of your website, the way your staff deal with complaints or the layout of your shop.

With your positioning in mind, think about **how** you...

- Interact with your customers
- Train your staff
- Package your product
- Help customers start using your product
- Answer the company phone
- Follow privacy laws
- Choose who to sponsor
- Organize a client dinner
- Act in social media
- Decide who will perform at your event...

True story: In August 2003 Harley-Davidson celebrated their 100th anniversary in Milwaukee, U.S. Who would they invite to perform at the concert?

The performer arrives...

25
ALL YOUR ACTIONS NEED TO BE DECENT TOO

The more relevant and important your brand is to people, the more your actions will get noticed – and get reactions.

When people have strong feelings about your brand, they pay attention to the news about you. They also have expectations and opinions, and they want to share those within their social circles.

People perceive their favourite brands like trusted friends and react accordingly when a brand falls short of their expectations, lets them down or – even worse – does something nasty. Their feelings about the brand change right there and then. Often forever.

Because even when people might forget what actually happened, they won't forget the feeling, the bad taste that's left.

In our connected world both positive and negative messages distribute faster and wider than ever before.

You need to be aware, and if you make a mistake, respond properly, act immediately and improve fast. Think of your brand as a decent human being and act like one.

When you accept your responsibility and apologize like a decent human being, people will acknowledge it.

When you respond to a disaster like a decent human being, people will appreciate it.

When you ask for help like a decent human being, people will offer you hugely valuable insights.

THINK OF YOUR BRAND AS A DECENT HUMAN BEING AND ACT LIKE ONE.

26
BRANDS ARE NOT FOREVER

ALL BRANDS WILL EVENTUALLY DIE. AND IF YOUR BRAND IS NAMED AFTER YOUR COMPANY, YOUR COMPANY WILL DIE WITH IT.

Brands and product categories are locked.

Category relevance drives brand relevance.

When the product category is new and growing, your brand grows with it.

When your brand is associated with a category that has evolved into something else or your product category is simply no longer relevant, then your brand will die with it.

The category shift from film to digital photography made Kodak go out of business. Kodak was the number one film camera brand and could not stretch to digital cameras in the mind of the consumers.

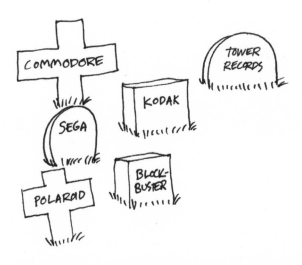

Similarly, when the move from traditional digital cameras to smart digital cameras happens, powered by Android for example, it will impact the leading traditional digital camera players Canon and Nikon. Both brands are strongly associated with their existing category, so they are likely to struggle to make the stretch. Canon and Nikon should establish new smart digital camera brands while they still can.

From all the Fortune 500 companies in 1955, a stunning 89% were gone in 2014. Give your company a different name from your brand, so when your brand dies, your company doesn't die with it.

Expand your business, not your brand.

27
DO NOT AVERT

To create a winning brand, you must synchronize everything discussed in this book, ensuring that your products and every action you ever take as a brand will always link back to the brand positioning.

Breaks between the positioning, products and actions will in the long run lead to consumer and employee confusion – and ultimately a meaningless brand.

When everything is truly in sync, you are continuously reinforcing the positioning of the brand in the mind of the consumer and strengthening its attachment to the product category.

Keep reminding people of your story and stay true to it, don't let it evaporate. It is the foundation of what you started – the essence of your brand.

KEEP TELLING YOUR STORY.

STAY IN SYNC.

ALWAYS.

STUBBORNLY.

CONSUMERS WILL LOVE

YOUR BRAND FOR IT.

**Get templates
and more insights at
theonlybrandbook.com**